Abraham and his wife Sarah, had many sheep. They also had herds of goats and fields of cattle and cute little pets to keep them company. Lots and lots of them.

But they had NO children. Their friends had children, lots of them. But Abraham and Sarah didn't even have one to call their own.

One day God gave Abraham a message, "Pack up all your things and go to a land that I will show you. I will be your guide."

It was a little bit scary to leave home and travel to a land he had never been to before. What if it's long? What if it's uncomfortable?

Abraham walked and then rested, and then walked some more. God said "Keep walking. You're almost there!" And so he continued.

Abraham, Sarah and all the animals finally arrived. "God has blessed us with a beautiful place!" Sarah told Abraham.

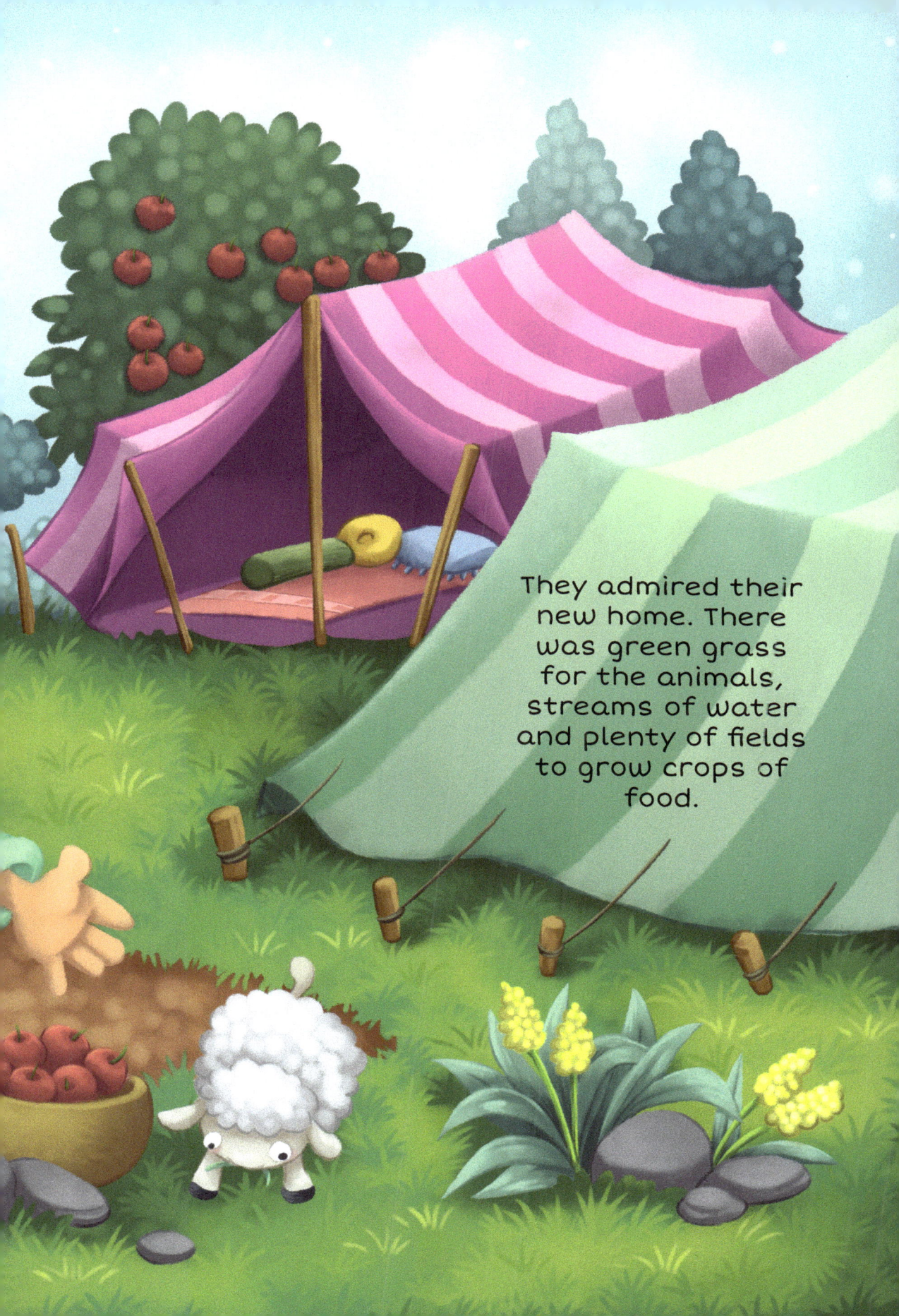

They admired their new home. There was green grass for the animals, streams of water and plenty of fields to grow crops of food.

"I will give you a son. He will have children, and his children will have children, and they will have children, as many as the stars in the sky."

It was a wonderful dream. But... just one small problem. My wife and I are way too old to have children now, Abraham thought. God saw Abraham's heart and replied, "I always keep My promises."

Abraham knew it was wise to listen to God, since He always knows best.

One day three men came to visit with a special message from God. "Sarah will have a son in only 9 months." they said. But Sarah was very old, way too old to have children.

Sarah heard this and laughed, for it was hard to believe such news.

God's promise came true after all, and Sarah had a baby boy. They named him Isaac. This little baby brought them so much joy.

Sometimes people are mean and they hurt each other. And that's what all the people were doing in two cities not too far from were Abraham lived.

But God wanted to keep His children safe. He sent the same visitors to get Abraham's cousin Lot, and his family out before the cities were destroyed.

It's not always easy to understand why God does some things. Abraham didn't understand some things either. But God can't do anything bad. He wanted Abraham to be so sure of this, so He gave him a test.

"Abraham, I want you to give Me back your son, Isaac." God said.

"What? You are asking me to give my only son? Isaac, that I waited for, for so long?" Abraham asked.

But Abraham knew that God was loving and good. He trusted God before and everything went well.

Difficult as it was, he decided to obey God's request, once again. God told him; "You have passed the test. And now, you may keep Isaac. Through him, I will continue to fulfill my promise to you!"

In the Bible, Abraham shows us many examples of faith and trusting God. Can you think of some ways you can practice faith and obeying God in your life today?

www.ingramcontent.com/pod-product-compliance
Lightning Source LLC
Chambersburg PA
CBHW040007080526
44586CB00027B/2911